CONTENTS

5 EASY STEPS TO SUCCESSFULLY HOMESCHOOL YOUR CHILD	3
Who is this book for?	5
1. Be patient and don't put too much pressure on yourself	7
2. Motivating your child to learn	10
3. Embrace technology	16
4. Let your child and their imagination take the lead	19
5. Making memorable experiences	23
BONUS: Put it to the test	27
References	31
Acknowledgements	33

5 EASY STEPS TO SUCCESSFULLY HOMESCHOOL YOUR CHILD

◆ ◆ ◆

Dedicated to all of the inspiring students who, despite a global pandemic, have continued to work hard and achieve their goals.

WHO IS THIS BOOK FOR?

  I am writing this book in 2020. A year of chaos, where many schools are closed for the indefinite future, with more children experiencing homeschooling than ever before. This is an uncertain and scary time for everyone, but it does not mean that your child and their education should suffer. This book will provide you with tips and tricks to help you teach your child at home, using strategies I have studied during my Psychology degree and implemented in classrooms catering to students of various age ranges. While I won't cover specific material, I will give you lesson structures and ideas that you can apply to any subject or topic you would like to focus on. Although the structure of your lessons is important, keeping your child motivated is another important factor of this experience that this book will focus on, as well as making sure that your lessons are as memorable and useful as possible.

This clear 5 step guide has been designed to be simple and easy to follow, ensuring that your child stays in the habit of learning something new every day, while not feeling overwhelmed and stressed by this unfamiliar learning experience and environment. This book aims to make the learning experience enjoyable for everyone involved. The last thing you want is to become overwhelmed with information to the point you feel underprepared and underqualified to take on this task.

At the end of the day, everyone only wants what is best for their children. By simply buying this book you have proven your dedication to your child and your desire for them to grow up to be a happy and healthy individual. Remember that every child is extremely unique in what motivates and drives them to want to learn. What one parent may find successful for their child, may not be the most effective and exciting method for your own child, and that's more than okay. This time with your child will help you learn more about them than you have ever known and will give you an exciting insight into how their mind works, discovers new things and most importantly how they use their creativity and imagination.

I will be taking you through some important steps and tools that teachers use to make their classes as engaging as possible so that learning does not become a monotonous task that your child will dread every day. We will be discussing how to set up your own home classroom, the psychological basis for memory and learning, and how to help your child succeed in their educational goals. Remember, you are not in this alone. While it may seem like a daunting task with a lot of responsibility placed on your shoulders, there are over 2 million children, all over the world, homeschooled each year. There is a very active online community filled with parents just like yourself, more than willing to offer their help and support, so don't be afraid to use all of the fantastic resources available.

1. BE PATIENT AND DON'T PUT TOO MUCH PRESSURE ON YOURSELF

Patience is a virtue. A home education may not be the norm for yourself or your children. A change in routine and environment can often be stressful for the whole family. As with anything, there will be a period of adjustment, so be prepared for this and try not to put too much pressure on yourself to have everything figured out right away.

It may be difficult to get your child to focus in their home environment. This is a space where they are used to playing with their toys and generally just being children after a day of learning at school. Therefore, it's important to set up separate areas for your child to distinguish between the tasks and expectations at hand. Ensuring that there is a desk or designated space that they can use for learning will be really useful for those who enjoy and thrive with a daily routine. While children who have sporadic bouts of motivation may benefit from having active areas all around your home, where they can enjoy a change in environment and activity often. However, keep in mind that homeschooling provides a terrific opportunity for your child to learn practical skills too, so don't feel confined to one workspace.

When creating a home classroom it is important that the area is inviting, colourful and fun. You could do this by decorating the space with pieces of art or work by your child, showing them that you are proud of their achievements. Having a display wall also works well as an incentive. Your child will want to work hard to have their creations on display, ready to show off to anyone willing to see.

This will not require anything particularly elaborate, but try to ensure that there are a range of different materials your child can use to create and carry out tasks. While a pencil and paper may be the norm in a traditional school, you want to ensure your set-up is as interactive and hands-on as possible to keep the motivation and desire to learn high. A timetable may also be an excellent idea for those who prefer a routine and can also be used as a superb motivator. Additionally, having a clock or timer next to your child while they work can be a great way of keeping yourself and your child focused on what you would like to achieve each day. For instance, If they know that they will have an hour of play-time if they work hard for the remaining 15 minutes, this can give them the extra push of motivation they need during a learning day.

The definition of learning is "the acquisition of knowledge". It's important not to box yourself in and limit the possibilities by defining home learning success only using measures such as conventional tests. Schools not only teach educational tools but also life skills. Doing activities such as cooking and baking may feel too fun to be classed as learning, but as long as your child is involved and leaves each activity having learned something new, you are doing a wonderful job.

Remember, children mirror the behaviours of those around them and are very good at picking up signals from their primary caregivers. If they notice that you are becoming stressed and worried when it comes to home-based learning, they will naturally imitate these emotions. This can decrease their motivation and desire to want to play, discover and create. If your homeschooling is temporary, for whatever reason, try not to worry too much about keeping your homeschooling experience too close to that of a traditional school experience. Teachers are well prepared to help children transition back into a traditional school day. While some parents may choose to take a hands-on approach, others may prefer to let their child dictate the day; there are no real right or wrong answers. Only you know what is best for your family at this time and no matter the extent of your home learning, teachers will be able to help solidify and add to this newfound knowledge when your child returns to school.

This may be the first time you are taking on the role of teacher. Remember, teachers have had years of experience in lesson planning and creating activities that they can often recycle year after year. While you may not have this advantage, you know your own child better than anyone. Don't overwhelm yourself with expectations of what you would like to achieve by the end of the day, week, or month. Children are nothing if not unpredictable, so try not to be demotivated if your ideas or activities are not going to plan.

2. MOTIVATING YOUR CHILD TO LEARN

There are many different psychological theories attempting to explain and promote motivation. One of the most prominent theories focuses on a concept called operant conditioning, conceived by distinguished psychologist Frank Skinner. Operant conditioning focuses on the use of rewards and punishments to promote long-term effects on behaviour.[1] There are two main levels to this theory, the first of which focuses on the variety of rewards and punishments that can be administered. While the second level examines the frequency in which these should be given in order to be effective.

Rewards, also referred to as reinforcements, come into play when positive and favourable behaviours are actively promoted. This can be done by either adding something your child enjoys or removing something they dislike. There can be either positive reinforcements or negative reinforcements. Positive reinforcement is when something is added to encourage a positive behaviour which has been carried out. For example, rewarding your child with their favourite snack when they do a great job. Whilst a negative reinforcement is when something that would generally be unfavourable to them, is removed to praise good behaviour or work. An example of this would be removing the number of chores your child has to do if they concentrate and do a good job on their homework.

Punishments, however, come into play when negative and unwanted behaviours are actively discouraged. During a positive punishment, something is added to decrease the likelihood of a certain behaviour taking place again. For example, increasing the number of chores your child has to do if they do not complete their homework. Whilst a negative punishment would be removing something that is favourable to discourage unacceptable behaviour. A common example of this would be limiting or completely revoking any time your child is allowed on a gaming device if they do not complete their homework.

Of the previously discussed four options, positive reinforcement has been found to be the most effective, with long-lasting results. This suggests that rewarding your child for working hard by adding something they enjoy into their day or lesson can be very motivating. This, in turn, should continuously motivate them to work hard and keep receiving these rewards.

There are many different ways you can implement positive reinforcements into the learning experience. Be creative with your rewards. They can be anything your child enjoys from an allotted amount of time on a gaming device, to some time to play outside or watch a movie. But ensure that reinforcements are only given when you want to encourage the behaviour your child has been exhibiting, as otherwise, this can become confusing for your child.

The second level of this theory investigates how often you should distribute these rewards to ensure the best results. You don't want to overwhelm your child with punishments or reinforcements to the point they lose their meaning or importance. Since positive reinforcement has been found to be the most effective, we will now discuss the different ways you can implement it, starting from least effective to most effective.

Continuous Reinforcement: This is when your child is awarded every time they carry out a desirable behaviour. It has been found that consistently reinforcing a favourable behaviour every time it is displayed actually decreases motivation and if reinforcements were to stop, the positive behaviour will quickly follow. As an example, if you were to give your child their favourite snack every time they finish a piece of work, they may quickly become desensitised to this reward. This small treat would rapidly become mundane and boring, which consequently would decrease their motivation and drive to work hard.

Fixed Ratio Reinforcement: This is when a positive behaviour is encouraged after a fixed number of times. For example, you can reward your child after every fifth completed homework. This is a great way to motivate your child, as the encouraged behaviour will continue for a significant amount of time. However, there are still even more effective patterns you can use.

Fixed Interval Reinforcement: This pattern is similar to that mentioned above. However, instead of being rewarded after carrying out a behaviour a certain number of times, they are rewarded after an allotted time period. An example of this is rewarding your child at the end of every lesson, day or week, if they have worked hard and actively been involved in their own learning.

Both fixed interval and fixed ratio reinforcement are more effective than continuous reinforcement, as it will take longer for your child to become desensitised towards the reward. These methods are also good because they give your child fixed and achievable goals that they can see in the near future and work towards.

Variable Ratio Reinforcement: This is when your child is randomly rewarded after displaying a positive behaviour. This pattern means that your child might be rewarded after completing five homeworks one week, but only after three homeworks the next week. As your child will not know when they are likely to receive a reward, this keeps their motivation levels strong, ensuring a high standard of work every time in the hope of a reward. Just make sure that the rewards don't become so sporadic that your child believes they are unlikely to be rewarded again. Variable ratio reinforcement has also been shown to have long-lasting effects on the positive behaviours it encourages.

Variable Interval Reinforcement: This pattern has been shown to have the highest effectiveness rate. Here your child is given rewards after random time periods of showcasing positive behaviour. For example, your child can be given a reward if they work for three hours one day, but only 50 minutes another day. This keeps motivation high as they are unsure of when the next reward will come, ensuring the encouraged behaviour will last for a long period of time. This can also be particularly useful for children who have intermittent bursts of motivation and find themselves completing more work on some days than others.

The main thing to take away from the subject of motivation is the importance of favourable behaviour and good work being rewarded in random time intervals, if possible. This keeps your child on their toes and will encourage them to produce exceptional pieces of work to a high standard, in the hope that their efforts will be recognised and they will be rewarded. While, on the other hand, a continuous stream of rewards can become meaningless very quickly, so try to avoid this habit.

While discussing the theme of motivation, feedback is another fantastic way to keep your child focused and on the right track. This helps to encourage and remind them that they are doing a good job. When giving feedback, it is really important to balance the good and the bad. An overwhelming amount of negative and constructive criticism can be disheartening. While an overflow of positive feedback can create a false sense of security. Here are some useful tips you can use when giving your child feedback on any project:

1. **Be specific.** Make sure that when giving your thoughts on any piece of work you are specific about what you enjoyed and what you believe they have done particularly well. This creates a sense of pride and will really emphasise to your child that they are being listened to.

2. **Balance the good and the bad.** Make sure to highlight your child's strengths whilst also making it clear to them what they would benefit from spending more time working on. If your child is constantly given only positive feedback, this

can become de-motivating very quickly. For example, many classrooms around the world use the 'two stars and a wish' framework. This is when your child is given two positive points about their work alongside one 'wish' which offers advice on points or techniques they may want to include in the future.

3. **Offer solutions.** Whilst it is important to highlight what your child needs to spend some extra time working on, you should also make it clear how they can work on this. This will help them envision a clear path to success with necessary steps. Make sure they always have attainable goals to work towards and that their hard work and effort is recognised when they reach their goals.

Finding out what specifically motivates your child will take some time and is a continuous process. As we have mentioned earlier children are great at mirroring behaviour, so try teaching them things that you are passionate about. This passion will shine through and when you are excited about a topic your child will hopefully share this enthusiasm with you.

3. EMBRACE TECHNOLOGY

In our modern world, technology is deeply ingrained in our everyday lives. Your child will grow up in a world where their technological proficiency could be critical to their job prospects and career options. You may be surprised by how much they already know and how quickly they pick up technological skills.

There are many online resources that are brilliant for developing computing skills, ranging from tools that teach your child how to create documents, presentations and spreadsheets, to the basics of programming languages. These skills are invaluable in today's world, with schools all over the globe implementing them into their curriculum. [2]

One tool that I have found to be particularly useful, for a wide range of ages, is 'Google Forms'. This is an online form creator that only requires a free Google account to access. It allows you to create a range of questions and collect answers in a multitude of formats. Once individuals have responded to your form, their responses are compiled and visualised using pie charts and diagrams. These charts are a useful way to incorporate an element of maths as you can practice converting your raw results into percentages or vice versa. To practice speaking and presenting skills, you could have your child present some of their findings back to you or other friends and family members. This is also a fantastic opportunity for them to work on building their confidence in public speaking, a valuable and transferable skill to have later in life.

Google Forms is also a great tool for psychology lessons. You and your child can carry out experiments by asking friends and family members a series of questions. Just like a real psychology experiment, you can hypothesise what your results will look like and how people will answer each of the questions. Once you have collected your responses using Google Forms you can compare your predictions to your final results.

Another great tool is 'Kahoot!'. This is an online quiz platform that is free and fun for everyone involved. There are pre-made lessons and quizzes available on any topic you can think of, and if there are no quizzes on the specific curriculum you are focusing on, you can easily make your own. If there is one thing I have learned from teaching, it is that most children thrive with competition. You can create challenges with your own Kahoot!'s and send the link to other parents in similar positions and compare scores. This is a good way of gauging how well your child has retained and understood a topic and creates some healthy competition.

You can also use technology to discuss countries of the world and different cultures with your child. Have you always wanted to travel somewhere but haven't had the chance or funds to go yet? Try using online resources such as 'Google Maps' and its street view function which allows you to take a virtual tour and 'walk' around the beautiful countries our world has to offer. This is also an opportunity to talk about landscapes, cultures and even learn some new words from the native language of the country you are 'visiting' by looking at street signs and advertisements. Children are very inquisitive and love to explore when given the opportunity to do so. Why don't you make the experience multisensory and try some of the food from your chosen country too? Make this activity your own and allow your child to guide the activity to keep them interested.

It's very important to showcase to your child how the skills they learn today will be beneficial for their future. By using these online tools to give your child a range of useful and employable skills, you are opening up a vast range of opportunities for their future. This may also help them determine what they enjoy doing and spark a passion for a particular career path.

4. LET YOUR CHILD AND THEIR IMAGINATION TAKE THE LEAD

It has been scientifically proven numerous times that multisensory experiences are always the most memorable and effective way to learn. [3] Think back to your childhood. You may not remember every day you spent sitting in a classroom listening to a teacher. But you will most likely remember the day you made slime as a science experiment or the day that a firefighter and their truck came to visit and show you how they did their job.

Multisensory experiences are much easier to do at home, due to the benefit of not being confined to a single classroom or school building. You can achieve multisensory experiences with a wide range of tasks, anything from stimulating your child's taste buds with cooking and baking to touching, smelling and exploring nature in your garden.

Getting them to engage and connect with all of their senses will create a memorable and enjoyable experience.

Physically standing up, moving and interacting with their materials has been proven to consolidate learning. This is because involving all senses creates multiple pathways that their neurons can use to recall this experience later down the line. This technique can be applied to any topic that you embark on with your child. For example, instead of just remembering the time they listened to someone talk about a species of flower, they can recall going to see the flower and remember what it smelled and felt like, allowing them to recollect and unlock more information from that time.

Social Cognitive Theory claims that a large majority of our learning comes from the social environment we are surrounded by. [4] In accordance with this theory, learning can occur during any activity whether your child is actively taking part or simply observing. This further emphasises my previous point that you should not feel pressure to conform to the normal routine and lesson structures that take place within schools. Being outside of a traditional school environment can be a huge advantage. It gives you much more of an opportunity to create diverse learning experiences controlled by your child, instead of being confined to the generic teacher-focused classroom.

Student-focused and -driven learning is becoming more popular and is widely adopted by teachers every year. Allowing students to take the lead when it comes to their learning increases their self-motivation and interest in each subject. [5] This can also be helpful when you are homeschooling multiple children, as each child will inevitably have different strengths and ability levels. Allowing your children to determine what they would like to learn and how they would like to learn, means that both children can progress and work on developing their own strengths and weaknesses whilst ensuring the other does not fall behind.

In a traditional school setting, students are often expected to passively learn by taking notes and following instructions. By allowing your child to take control of their own education, with your guidance, you are allowing them to have a more active role in their own learning. You can practice student-focused learning by asking your child about what interests them. Once they have decided on a topic, you can provide them with lots of tools and research skills to explore and find more information by themselves. This style of learning gives your child more independence and develops their ability to find answers on their own, instead of relying on educators to provide solutions for them. To help your child in this method of education, try presenting them with questions they can explore to keep their research focused. For example, if your child expresses a desire to learn about South America, you could suggest that they research a traditional dish from each of the countries and try making it at home.

Children who follow student-focused learning methods often report that they are more motivated and satisfied with their learning experience. This will also create trust within your relationship, by showing your child that you trust them to take the reign of their own learning.

Having these skills will be beneficial for your child should they decide to continue onto further education. In a university or college setting, students are expected to be extremely self-sufficient and take charge of their own studies. By following student-focused learning your child will be well equipped for this challenge.

5. MAKING MEMORABLE EXPERIENCES

In this chapter, we will discuss various memory techniques that your child can use to enhance their recall and retention abilities. This will ensure that the information and skills they are learning at home now will stay with them for life.

Something we will discuss extensively is memory cues. These cues come in a variety of forms, usually linked to at least one of the five senses, and can trigger our memories making them very useful in the process of learning. They could be anything from a smell that your child associates with the material, to a sound that they remember hearing when first learning the topic. These seemingly small cues can help our brain piece together memories and retrieve previously learned information.

As we have previously discussed, multi-sensory experiences create various neural pathways which increase the number of ways in which we can recall information. This is because there are numerous cues that your child can use to retrieve the information from their memory bank.

For example, instead of solely relying on remembering what they have heard about a science experiment, they can recall back to the day they did it. From here they can remember the smell that filled the room or what colour the chemicals were. Having hands-on and visually striking experiences creates more cues to help them remember the information that was learned.

It's also important to keep in mind that there are cues all around us. Multiple studies have shown that you are more likely to succeed in a test taken in the same room that you initially learned the information, compared to a test taken in a new environment. This is because cues in the room can potentially trigger memories. Therefore, it may be beneficial to ensure that your child has a dedicated workspace for learning, separate to where they play, so they can utilise any potential triggers in their home classroom when taking tests. Similar methods which your child can use include studying in the same clothes they will wear to an exam, writing with the same pen, or wearing the same perfume to trigger their memory. The same effect can be seen when information is learned and tested at roughly the same time of day. This may be due to a similar mindset, level of concentration, or because your child is recalling information around the same time they initially learned it. This highlights the potential advantages of having a structured timetable. [6]

Acronyms are another useful memory technique that your child can practice. These are made-up words that relate back to the information you are trying to remember. For example, 'ROY G BIV' - is a widely used acronym to remember the colours of the rainbow in order - **R**ed, **O**range, **Y**ellow, **G**reen, **B**lue, **I**ndigo, and **V**iolet. To increase the effectiveness of the acronym, make sure that it is meaningful to your child. For instance, if you wanted to remember the three types of blood vessels (**A**rteries, **C**apillaries and **V**eins), consider using the names of your child's friends such as '**A**my, **C**hloe, and **V**anessa' instead of arbitrary words like '**A**dventure, **C**amel, and **V**ampire'.

Mind maps are also a powerful memory technique if your child is particularly strong at picturing things in their imagination. You can create a mind map by drawing a spider diagram with branches of interconnected information sprouting out from the centre of the page. Make sure your mind maps are as colourful as possible, as it gives your child multiple ways to recall information. For example, if your child is having trouble remembering something, using this technique may aid them as they can picture the relevant mind map in their head and imagine both the position of the information on the page and what colour it is written in, providing alternative neural pathways to access this information.

Linking information to topics and subjects that your child has previously learnt about, and has particular strengths in, will also lessen the difficulty of retrieving new information. It's important to show your child that what they are learning is not only applicable to one subject or area of knowledge but can be used throughout multiple areas. Similarly, if your child is struggling to grasp a particular concept, it may be beneficial for you to link this with another topic that they understand well. This will allow your child to relate information from the topic that they already understand, and apply it to the concept that they are struggling with.

To conclude, there are a wide range of memory techniques

that can be used to enhance recall and retention abilities. I encourage you to try each of the discussed methods with your child and see which works best for them. But remember that everyone is different. So don't get discouraged if your child doesn't like a particular strategy or it's not very effective for them. Some other psychology-based memory techniques that you can read about online and try with your child include the method of loci, spaced repetition, and active recall.

BONUS: PUT IT TO THE TEST

Understandably, you will want to ensure that your child has understood, and is able to use, the concepts that you discuss and learn about at home. This can be done using a variety of different methods. In this bonus chapter, I will discuss how to use some techniques, outlined in Bloom's Taxonomy, to test your child's progress beyond the conventional testing methods used in the majority of schools.

Bloom's Taxonomy is a set of three education models that are used to outline learning objectives. The most popular of these three models is the cognitive model. This outlines six ordered cognitive abilities which each subsequently lead to a higher-order of thinking. [7]Higher-order thinking generally leads to a more sophisticated thought process beyond simply recalling or understanding information. The most important part of this model is ensuring that your child is confident with the previous skill before they move onto the next, as each skill builds upon the last. Here are the six levels of abilities and how they can be used to test your child's progress. For this example, let's assume your child is learning about the different types of IQ tests.

1. Retaining Knowledge - This is the fundamental ability needed to form all other skills, as you cannot understand, apply, or analyse information you don't remember. Try using some of the techniques from the previous chapter to help with memory skills. For example, your child could use an acronym to help them remember the different types of IQ tests.

2. Understanding - When your child is at this stage they can fully comprehend what they have remembered. A great way to implement and check their understanding is by asking them to rewrite or summarise the information in their own words. At this stage, you could ask your child to define an IQ test and summarise the different types.

3. Application - By this point your child should be able to apply their new-found knowledge to novel situations in order to solve problems. You can make this stage as hands-on as you prefer, with tasks ranging from small "what would you do" scenarios to practically applying the new knowledge they have acquired. Here, your child could administer a well-known IQ test to friends and family members.

4. Analysing - After becoming confident in applying their knowledge your child can move onto the analysing stage. During analysis, your child can organise and relate their new knowledge to theories they already hold. This can be done by discussing how their current topic relates to those

they have previously studied. As we have already discussed, this will also help with ingraining the information into their knowledge bank. To analyse IQ tests, your child could research why we may need them and when it would be necessary to use them.

5. Evaluating - This next step can range from your child evaluating the effectiveness of their new knowledge, to finding evidence to support or argue against it. In our example, your child could compare and investigate each test and argue which of them is most effective and why.

6. Creation - The sixth ability focuses on your child using the skills that they have built in the previous steps to create an original piece of work. To review your child's progress at the highest-order of thinking, you can ask them to come up with a new idea based on their knowledge. To conclude our example, you could ask your child to create their own IQ test and explain the different elements of it to you.

Mastering each of these abilities will help your child build skills towards a higher-order of thinking. This is a great skill to have in life and will ensure they can logically tackle any new information or problems that come their way in an organised manner.

Whichever way you chose to benchmark your child's progress, it is best to plan ahead and have your preferred method in mind when initially teaching them the subject. Knowing how you will be evaluating their progress and giving them the essential tools they need to meet your expectations is a valuable practice to keep in mind. Backwards planning is a technique used by many teachers and is very useful for ensuring that the objectives that you have for a particular topic are met at every stage of learning, setting your child upon the road to success.

While in this book we have discussed a wide variety of tools and techniques that can be used to successfully home-school your child, I would love to emphasise my earlier point that each child is unique. Although these techniques are based on psychological theories, this does not mean they are the only "correct" answer. Only you know what is truly best for your child. I wish you all the best on your homeschooling journey.

◆ ◆ ◆

"There is no school equal to a decent home and no teacher equal to a virtuous parent" - Gandhi

REFERENCES

[1]Segers, E., Beckers, T., Geurts, H., Claes, L., Danckaerts, M., & van der Oord, S. (2018). Working memory and reinforcement schedule jointly determine reinforcement learning in children: Potential implications for behavioral parent training. Frontiers in Psychology, 9.

[2]Jagušt, T., Botički, I., & So, H. -J. (2018). A review of research on bridging the gap between formal and informal learning with technology in primary school contexts. Journal of Computer Assisted Learning, 34(4), 417–428.

[3]Baines, L. (2008). A Teacher's Guide to Multisensory Learning: Improving Literacy by Engaging the Senses. ASCD.

[4]Schunk, D. H. (1), & DiBenedetto, M. K. (2). (n.d.). Motivation and social cognitive theory. Contemporary Educational Psychology, 60.

[5]Cunha, R. S., Ribeiro, L. M., Sequeira, C., Barros, R. de A., Cabral, L., & Dias, T. S. (2020). What makes learning easier and more difficult? The perspective of teenagers. Psicologia Em Estudo, 25.

[6]Rair, R. J. (2019). Test Environment for Optimal Performance in high school students: Measure development and the relationship with standardized test scores (Doctoral dissertation, Kent State University).

[7] Anderson, L.W., Krathwohl, D.R., & Bloom, B.S. (2000). A Taxonomy for Learning, Teaching, and Assessing: A Revision of Bloom's Taxonomy of Educational Objectives.

ACKNOWLEDGEMENTS

I am forever grateful to my wonderful boyfriend, friends and family for supporting me in every adventure and task I take on. I cannot thank them enough for their moral support and proof-reading skills. I love you all very much. I would also like to thank the incredible teachers and young people I have worked with over the years who have taught me so much and shown me an unbelievable amount of kindness.

Printed in Great Britain
by Amazon